Caught on Site
(Confessions from the Trade)
by Dennis Swift
ISBN: 978-0-9954805-6-8

Cover design and illustration by BazMac

Published by

i2i Publishing. Manchester.
www.i2ipublishing.co.uk

Introduction

Building sites can be a mucky place especially during the Winter months when puddles of water and mud are everywhere. It was also hard work plastering as you seldom got to see much of your fellow-colleagues, as everyone was spread out, so there was very limited time for socialising.

Working on new build was so repetitive; mixing plaster and spreading it on the walls, boarding out ceilings was also a nightmare. Those eight by four sheets were heavy and needed two people. I believe now they have a machine that raises the boards into place before fixing to the joists.

I always recall my first visit to the USA where I stumbled upon a building site. It was fascinating watching the differences in practice compared to ours. I watched two Mexican lads board out a ceiling in only a few minutes. A lifting machine took the boards to the ceiling and these lads used a nail gun to fix them. They were also wearing stilts, something Health & Safety would prevent in the UK. Here in the UK, we continued using galvanised nails and a hammer, we got there but it was hard graft.

New build was getting harder and a fortunate break saw me working on social housing. BS Heating wanted a plasterer to patch plaster where electricians had rewired, this was a doddle compared to full walls and ceilings. This is where I met some of the craziest characters whose antics had you in stitches. I worked for a couple more companies that offered me a similar type of work but it was Durose & Gourlay where I met most of the characters featured in this book.

I have been tempted many times to write a book about these characters but no one would probably believe what they read. I can assure you that the contents of this book are almost 100% true and the people do or did exist.

About the Author

I was born in December 1955 to parents Joseph and Mary. I had a brilliant up-bringing and lived with them until I met my wife to be.

I was 19 when I met Brenda, we got married a few years later and together we have three children now grown-up. We have been Married for thirty-eight years and some tell me she deserves a medal for putting up with me. I will buy her one as soon as I find time.

I'm now a retired Plasterer suffering from Osteoarthritis in both knees which restricts my activities. This has given me the time to write, "Caught on Site. Confessions from the Trade" and my previous book `Football Rhymes of Passion`

I'm a Bolton Wanderers fan and season ticket holder for too many years to mention, however, I relinquished my ticket last season as I'd had enough of watching poor football which at times got me so frustrated.

I've been lucky enough to be flown down to Sky Sports studios in Isleworth near London, to represent Bolton Wanderers on *Fanzone*. This is where two fans of different teams sit together in a studio and commentate on the game which is broadcasted live. It's an interesting alternate to the usual commentary! I did this on many occasions.

I've also appeared on an ITV Digital football quiz show called *Did I Not Know That* hosted by Simon O`Brien and more recently ITV *Tipping Point* hosted by Ben Shepherd. Both shows, I returned home empty handed.

Another of my passions is Real Ale. I love the different flavours of these traditionally brewed beers. I'm also a massive fan of the Micro-Breweries producing Craft Ale as well as the lovely foreign beers.

My home town of Atherton has quite a decent selection of real ale pubs attracting beer drinkers from other neighbouring towns. Once every year the beer bash arrives in town.

Dennis Swift.

Testimonials

Denn's experience on building sites and in property repairing have furnished him with a fund of stories about the scrapes and japes he has got into over the years.

You will meet a wealth of characters he has worked with such as Moonshine Bill who blew up three sheds in his pursuit of the perfect home brewed liquor!

He will tell you about some of the filthy houses he has worked in and the strange objects that have been found – sometimes of a sexual nature.

You will also learn why it is unwise to hold a full bag of plaster over your head or let Denn anywhere near your chimney.

If you only learn one thing from this funny little book, it will be why it is a good idea to put a strong lock on your knicker drawer! I'll say no more.

Dave Dutton Actor and Author. www.davedutton.co.uk

If you think some of these stories are made up, then I'm here to tell you they would have happened. I know, because I'm related to a former housing officer of 25 years standing, and can confirm that such goings on... actually went on. Read on and enjoy!

Bernard Wrigley Singer Actor & Comedian
www.bernardwrigley.com

Reading through the transcript copy of 'Confessions from the trade...caught on site', we came to realise that most folk who has ever worked for a living, will have some cracking stories to tell. The trick is to write them down before you forget any of the juicy detail.

Dennis has proverbially 'hit the nail on the head' with these memoirs. Our songs are exactly the same, stories that the good folk of Wigan have recalled, and they have simply just been put to music.

Dennis' tales here are a testament that you do not need to wander far to find pure entertainment by either your work colleagues or your clients. And it is very gratifying to see some poor bugger come a cropper, and that said individual's antics had just contributed another few pages to the book!

Prepare to have your eyes opened by what goes on in the humble trade of the Tradesman!
You just couldn't make it up!

Les Hilton & Tim Cooke from Chonkinfeckle
www.chonkinfeckle.co.uk/

Contents

Something Fishy

There are characters in every profession but the Building trade seems to have the best. Every company employs them and there are certain ones who always bear the brunt of the jokes.

Gary Hollinshead was no exception. He was a real target for the pranksters and his reactions always had us in stitches with laughter. For some strange reason, his nickname was 'Gash'!! Not too sure why. Gash drove the pickup truck and was one of a many store-persons employed by the company. He was always a happy lad but soon got stressed and had many tantrums.

One particular day, one of the lads thought of a great way to get Gash going; he bought a fish from a local market and waited for him to disappear for a while. Gash was cleaning out one of the cabins and left the pickup truck unlocked. This lad crept into the cab, undid one of the panels and placed the fish behind it. At first, Gash never noticed anything different but did mention it to one of the lads on the site that there was a strange smell in the pickup.

The Foreman was in on this and asked Gash, "What is that smell in your pickup Gary?"

"It's not me," replied Gary but there's a strange smell in the truck.

Each day that went by the smell became a worse stench but Gary had no idea it was a dead fish. The foreman kept telling Gary to get that pick up cleaned out because it stinks. Gary got really upset and was on about this smell all the time telling everyone there was a strange smell coming from the cab. Certain people whom Gash mentioned this to ran away howling with laughter knowing that this stunt would be a classic.

After a few days, the stench got worse, it was also rather warm and Gash would use the blower on the pick up to keep cool whilst driving. The air blowing into the cab was pure smelly fish which now had him at desperation stage. He had cleaned the entire cab and sprayed polish on the dash board and bought air fresheners in the hope of getting rid of the smell.

Each time anyone walked past the truck Gary would be sitting there scratching his head, shouting to everyone passing that he couldn't understand the stench and where it was coming from. We couldn't go anywhere near because we would crack up, just at Gary's emotions. It was only later when Gary was on his dinner break that he decided to inspect behind the panels and then found what the stench was. He removed it and demanded to know who was behind it. I'm not too sure if he ever did find who was responsible.

There are more adventures with Gash further on in the book.

Peter's Vacation

Peter was a Storeman and drove the pickup truck, he also had the nickname 'spaced out' because he always seemed as if he was a million miles away. Whilst on the site he would sort out the tools and materials for the trades people and be on hand should anyone need assistance. Peter would eye all the women up and would know exactly where they all lived.

Once he'd sorted out the lads he'd sit in the truck watching and waiting. He would sometimes say to a few of the lads in his soft toned voice, "there's a nice little sweetie at that house." Sometimes he would chat with them and tell the lads, "I think I'm in here".

Pete got friendly with one lady and word got around quite quickly regarding this, especially in the site office. The woman Peter fancied, had been seeing her ex-husband for a while but nothing had materialised from it. The woman was talking to Les who was the site foreman; she mentioned that she was going to Torquay for a week as her ex was down there and he'd booked a Hotel for the week.

Peter came into the site office with a smile on his face that day. He mentioned that this particular lady was going to Torquay for a week and she said, "You can take me if you want". He was chuffed to bits about this and asked to book a week off work in the belief she would be with him. Les knew about this but he never mentioned to Peter that she was going to meet her ex.

Peter always got the wrong message and told the lads he was going to Torquay for a week with this lady and they were going next week. No one said a word to Peter that they knew about her going to see her ex.

Peter packed his case and placed it in the boot and collected the young lady. Once down in Torquay and in front of the Hotel, Peter got the cases from the boot, put them down and closed the lid.

She said to Peter, "And where do you think you're going." Pete was gob smacked by this because the lady was meeting her ex Husband. Pete had to drive all the way back but he even went back down to pick her up.

Whilst on another site, this time in Rochdale, Peter was with Les once again. The site office was in a unit on an industrial estate. Les was always a wind-up merchant who was always laughing and joking. Les just happened to mention, whilst Peter was in the site office, knowing that he would bite, saying that two stunning women just drove past in a convertible BMW and said that they went into a TV shop in one of the units.

Peter clocked this and was listening very carefully, "I think they must be making blue movies in there," said Les!

At dinner time Peter was nowhere to be seen, it was only later when he was asked by one of the lads, "what was you doing parked up in front of that TV place?"

Apparently, the unit was a TV repair shop and these two women must have gone to another unit but they had parked their BMW in front of the TV repairs. Another failure for poor Pete.

The New Site

As one contract came to an end we'd all be wondering where we would be deployed next. The company had no preferences who went where and when, even if it meant a thirty or a forty-mile journey through the early morning rush hour to get to the site in time to start. Sometimes we'd get lucky and land on a local job, these were the best which meant less fuel and more time to yourself.

The new site I was assigned to was in Blackburn, tiling kitchens. This was a simple job and took me only a few hours to complete. Kev who was foreman was great bloke (only pity he was a Man U fan and was always rabbiting on how good his team were.) I always got great pleasure going in Monday mornings when his beloved Man U had lost and better still when it was my team Bolton who beat them. This did happen, but not very often.

When I arrived on site for the first time I presumed I'd be plastering the chases in the walls and ceilings where the electricians had rewired. Kev showed me the property I would be working in which required plastering after the electricians had rewired. The contract had only just begun and I had been brought in early as the plasterer who would be working on this site was completing his work on a site elsewhere.

Everything was like clockwork, the old kitchen was ripped out and stripped on day one, next came the electricians, the day after were the kitchen fitters, plasterer day after, then the tiler. I plastered the first kitchen and the second one but was told I was to be tiling the kitchens at one per day. One thing for sure Kev got everything well organised from the labourers to the truck driver/storeman whose job it was to clean up and sort out the materials ready for the next day.

I was not qualified as a tiler, but there was really nothing to tiling a kitchen. Each kitchen was almost the same apart from the odd couple. Each tenant of the house got to choose their colour of kitchen and tiles to match. I must admit there were a few weird choices.

After completing the first tiling job I'd done in years, I cleaned up and left the site this was the norm as it was job and knock as they called it.

Next day Kev was waiting for me to arrive. I was always early so I got a bollocking whilst no one else was in the office. I had not cleaned the work surface properly and once the grout had dried left the surface all powdery. I was asked to return to the house and apologise to the tenant who actually was a good sport and accepted my apology. I knew from now on I had to leave the surfaces to dry then wipe everything down with a dry cloth. It did take me an extra half hour but the quality of the workmanship was there for all to see.

This contract was great especially during the summer months where everything seemed more pleasant. One tenant did give me a problem and he was an Asian guy who was standing behind me watching every move I made. He was joined by a few others who drew up their chairs and asked questions as each tile was fixed. Even the electric cutting machine I used was moved by one young guy who began cutting a tile. I found it so funny as the water guard was raised and sprayed this lad with white creamy liquid as he pressed the on button. I gave him a stern warning not to touch any of the machinery and ordered them out of the kitchen. They refused to leave so I called for Kev to come around.

Kev came sauntering in and asked the tenant to put the kettle on, Kev even joined them and called me a lazy git and told me to get on with it. I shook my head and laughed. This kitchen took me all damn day and gave a tiling lesson to four Asians who probably now or have been posing as tilers thanks to my tuition.

The little old lady

One day the house I was to tile was a very posh house and I was instructed to use plenty clean dust sheets, not that all the other properties were dirty.

The tenant was an elderly Irish lady who greeted me at 8 AM who said, "Before you begin would like a Fecking cup of tea!!! I was taken back by her question and pretended

I didn't hear her the first time so she said again but in a much sterner voice, "Would you like a Fecking cup of tea." I said I would love one. Now one thing with us trades people we tend not to sit down and drink the tea but we have a sip now and again.

The Irish lady reminded me that my tea was going cold by saying, "drink your Fecking tea before it goes cold." She reminded me a few times before telling me she won't be making me any more fecking cups of tea. The language was most colourful from a lady of her age but, according to form, it was a normal everyday word used by Irish folk? I'm not too sure of that.

Les Potter was the foreman on a job in Leigh Lancashire and Les loved a good laugh.

I'd only been on this site for a few days and was still finding my way around. Les asked me to visit a property to finish off a bit of plastering around a doorframe that had been fitted. I was given the address but before I left Les said! "Denn! when you go there don't laugh when the lady opens the door."

I asked, "Why! Les told me, "You'll understand when she opens the door because she looks a bit like Jim Bowen from bullseye." Les also said I was the last person he'd really want to go there but there was no other plasterer.

I knocked on the door until the lady answered. I burst out laughing as she stood there at the opened door. She asked me what's tickled me? Which made me laugh even more. I told her I'd be back in a few mins after I picked up some sheets to put down.

On my return to the cabin, Les asked, "You didn't laugh, did you?"

I just said, "super great smashing."

I was sent to a Site in Bury that was way out in the wilds and not easy to get to during the morning rush.

I was paired up with Neil to board out ceilings and re-plaster the walls in kitchens. Whilst we were finishing off the ceiling a shout of "Neil" came from outside this property that we were working in. It was Andrew the contracts manager who came on site to pay us a visit but wanted Neil because his Van had been damaged whilst parked outside this property.

Andrew came into this property and said to Neil, "Your Van 'as just been run into!"

Neil then asked in a stern voice, "Did you get a description of who did it?"

"I sure did," said Andrew struggling not to laugh. "It's got a long snout a pair of pointed ears and it shits a lot"?

This baffled Neil who found out exactly what ran into his Van. Two Police horses were strolling down the road when one must have been frightened and sat on the bonnet of Neil's Van. The other officer on horseback asked Neil for his documents, I won't repeat what his reply was.

Whilst on another Wigan site Kev was once again the leader of the merry men. He always seemed to get lumbered with the same characters but Kev never bothered as the work always got done professionally.

Angy was at the centre of attention once more when he decided to sneak off site early. Brian the contracts manager happened to see Angy standing at the Bus Stop and decided to confront him the following morning.

The very next day Brian came into the cabins and said to Angy, "You are docked half day's pay for yesterday."

"Why," said Angy?

Brian said, "I saw you at the Bus Stop yesterday lunchtime."

Angy replied instantly saying, "That was my twin brother, he saw me and came for a chat and went home around dinner time."

Brian said, "Don't give me that rubbish."

Angy then turned to both Banny and Jordy to back him up. Both of them agreed that Angy had a twin.

Brian's face was a picture as he didn't know whether to dock his wages or not.

Foreman Kev backed him by saying that he did have a twin Brother. Brian was convinced and left the cabin. Kev said, "You owe me a Breakfast for that," so on Friday they agreed to go for a Breakfast.

Friday came and they went off they went for their Breakfast.

Angy said, "I know a cracking place for a Breakfast," so off they set to a transport café not too far from the site. Kev had asked the Clerk of Works to come along. When they got there the place didn't seem nice, the cook was walking around the café with a cig in his mouth, his nails were long and dirty. He also took the orders.

When the food arrived the café owner carried the plates in one by one and a bit of ash landed on one plate. All plates and food were swimming in fat. They all began giving Angy some grief for suggesting this place.

Angy said, "What do you want for four quid?" It was enough for Kev and the Clerk of works who decided to walk out.

Sooty and Sweep

Everyone makes mistakes but accidents can be avoided like the time a simple job turned into a nightmare. A housing estate in Chorley was the venue of some funny happenings and this day was to be one of them.

Just another day on the site and another assignment. My job was to sweep the chimneys to enable a flu liner to be dropped down and re-plaster the area where the old fireplace was removed. It was a dirty job but I did keep the soot to a minimum by keeping the opening well sealed whilst I put the rods up the chimney. All was going well, apart from my hands getting covered in soot.

A guy they called Clint had a great idea how to go about sweeping the chimney. His proposed method was to sweep it from the top so all the soot would not fall on top of myself and make a mess. I began to think his idea actually made sense. Dust sheets would be duck taped to the wall covering the opening and sealed onto the hearth thus making it dustproof. I will never forget the old lady of the house sitting in her chair knitting. She was a very smart lady with white hair slightly tinted blue wearing a white cardigan. What happened next almost got me the sack.

After sealing the opening I took the brushes and rods up the Scaffolding ladder to the roof and began to send the brushes down the chimney, this was so easy compared to sweeping up and getting covered in soot. As I attached the last rod I gave it one big push then began to remove them one by one until the last rod with the brush attached came out of the stack. I gathered the rods tied them up and came down the ladder. This time, I was almost clean but for a slight dusting around the hands. Feeling a glow of satisfaction after making it so simple I went inside the house where I had a massive shock!! The lady was still knitting but she looked like a black silhouette. The sheet I taped to the wall had been displaced and the entire room had been engulfed in soot, I didn't know what to do whether laugh or cry, I think I did both.

I had to report the matter and even the foreman couldn't stop laughing when he saw what had happened. He said he would have to report it and bring one of the bosses to inspect the damage. The lady was moved to a local residential home for a couple of nights until her home was cleaned and suitable for living in once more. The next twenty or so houses the chimneys were professionally cleaned. I got a rocket but the company did see the funny side. I survived to see the contract out but never went near a chimney again.

Moonshine Bill

Housing estates are home to many characters and this person who we re-named Moonshine Bill was no exception. He brewed wine but then distilled it in his shed at the bottom of his garden.

Bill and his wife were both retired but seemed to keep themselves busy.

It was around September when we got to Bill's house but we'd seen him and his wife many times walking their dog and carrying plastic bags. One of the lads happened to have mentioned they had seen him rummaging through the bushes picking blackberries and Elderberries from the trees. He was asked what he did with them but all he said was they made pies and jams.

When it was their house to undergo refurbishment, Bill hadn't emptied his pantry as this was to be demolished to make the kitchen bigger. I remember the labourers saying at the time they'd moved loads of demi johns and bottles upon bottles of what seemed like wine.

The labourers were first in but normally at dinner time everyone converged back in the site office for their lunches and brews but this day there was no sign of them. One of the lads later found out that they'd all been fed with Apple and Blackberry pies washed down with wine and Beer. One of the labourers was absolutely stoned and was staggering around and eventually fell over. Good job the site foreman never saw him else he'd have been sent home, or if reported he could have lost his job. Everyone that visited Bill's that afternoon was singing and laughing and had to leave their car there on the site because they'd drank so much. He managed to get a lift to where he lived.

Everyone laughed when Bill's house was mentioned and those whose turn it was to work there, were told to be careful what they're given as they may not be driving home.

It was my turn to visit Moonshine Bill's and I wasn't disappointed. Sure, I got the Apple and Blackberry pie for dinner and I was also asked if I wanted a beer or Wine or even something stronger. I did say if he wanted me to sample anything I would take it home. I mentioned I made Wines and Beers but nothing any stronger, I told him I was interested in what he made that was stronger. He winked at me and said follow me to my Distillery.

After I had completed my work I followed him to his shed and what I saw was amazing. He'd made a complete distillery from copper piping and kettles. He also had a Burco boiler and several other homebrew implements. His 8x6 shed was full of beer, wines and spirits and much more fermenting in buckets and demi johns.

I took home with me that evening a few beer bottles, a bottle of wine and Bill's Moonshine which had been made from fruit collected last year. I can vouch they were some of the best home-brew Beers I'd tasted and his wine was simply fantastic. I sampled the spirit but that was like drinking methylated spirits but fruity. I actually poured some on a board and put a match to it, it did ignite.

The next day I paid him a visit to compliment him on his brews. To this day, I will never know how and what ingredients were used, apart from fruit and how he made them.

Whilst work was being carried out on the other houses in that vicinity everyone mentioned how we'd gone on in Bills! Apparently, he'd three sheds before the one he currently had, each blew up causing damage to nearby properties. That must have been a direct result of his experimentations before he perfected it. Well done Bill.

Works Outing

I was contacted by an agency who wanted a plasterer to finish off some work in Atherton. This came at the right time as work was drying up. I accepted and started the following day. It was only five mins from my home which was great. The company was from Wigan.

The lads on site were easy to get along with but there seemed little organisation as sometimes there were four or five different trades people in the house at once. A couple of the lads I knew from other companies I subbed for, but there were also quite a few to get to know.

The job lasted around four weeks and during that time the conversations at dinner time were mainly football and beer.

There was a huge guy named Dave who always listened but seldom said much. One day he said, "What's this real ale lark?" I mentioned to him it was good beer and that he should come out one night. A few of the lads were up for a night out and asked why I always went to Manchester. Dave was intrigued by this real ale as all he drank was lager.

I said to Dave "come out on Friday night and you'll enjoy it." Dave agreed.

On the Friday at dinner, Dave was listening to all the conversations regarding people's favourite beers some of which Dave had never heard of. "Do they sell Lager in these pubs?" Everyone began to laugh but Dave got a bit upset thinking they were having a go at him.

Dave stood up and in a stern voice said, "I'll come tonight and drink this real ale you keep going on about but if I'm ill Saturday morning you're all in for it Monday."

We all met up Victoria Station and headed for the first of many pubs. Dave mentioned he'd never been to Manchester before, especially for beers.

The first pub was one of my favourites called the `Pot of Beer,' a small pub not too far from the station.

Dave asked the bar man, "Where's the lager?"

The barman told him they were there!

"What the hell is that?" Dave said in a high voice.

I had to interrupt and mentioned to Dave they are Belgian Lagers; they didn't sell Fosters in there.

Dave reluctantly ordered a pint of what I was drinking which was a Hoegaarden and said it was brewed in a town by the same name.

"Urghhh, it's cloudy I'm not supping that." But after a while, I noticed his glass was almost empty. I asked him was it ok, Dave replied with a smile, "Aye it was alright".

The next pub was Marble Arch on Rochdale Rd, a micro-brewery pub that offered some great ales. Dave was asking if they sold that cloudy beer as he liked it. I had to explain that the beers in there were mainly their own. I suggested he try a Ginger Marble, a bitter which had hints of Ginger. Again, Dave was checking his pint closely and began to drink it. I'd not even got mine as Dave was queueing at the bar again. Dave seemed to be drinking two to my one.

By the time the evening was over and we had to get to the Station to catch the train home, Dave had supped twice as many as myself and the other three guys. He was belching loudly and staggering down the road saying, "If I'm bad tomorrow, you're all in for it on Monday."

I got to work on Monday morning hoping Dave was ok by Saturday morning. Dave arrived and came into the site office smiling.

He never mentioned Friday night until it was brought up by one of the other lads. "Smashing night out that were, when is the next" Dave enjoyed Manchester that much he visited the same pubs the following week.

When the job came to an end I never saw Dave again but I saw one of the lads who knew him well. He told me that he had become a regular in the pubs in the Northern quarter of Manchester and that he'd met a woman and now lives in that area.

Goes to show, "Don't knock it till you have tried it"

Gullible

Scott was a joiner and a likable lad who did whatever he was asked to do but he was very gullible. He always had a smiling face because nothing seemed to bother him. He worked his way up from a site joiner to a site supervisor.

It was whilst he was on the tools that he gave us such a laugh. His Father was the Health and Safety man for the company but Scott had his own ideas as to how the jobs should be done.

It was on a House refurbishment scheme in Wigan. A Van was parked up outside one of the properties that were being refurbished. A bloke got out of the van and began asking if anyone wanted to buy ten CD's?

Before he could finish the sentence, Scott said, "I'll have them," without even knowing what they were. Scott wanted the lot as he wasn't letting anyone make a profit apart from himself. He bought all ten.

Next day it was mentioned, "what was those CD's you bought yesterday Scott?"

"Oh," he said, "Does anyone want to buy them."

The lads began asking why he wanted to sell them.

Scott said, "Two were the same and one was aboriginal gospel music."

Les said to him, "You wouldn't sell that if you stood at the bottom of Ayers Rock!" Everyone was rolling over laughing.

A few mins later his Dad arrived on site and saw everyone laughing. Les who was supervisor couldn't wait to tell him what he bought.

His Dad began asking, "Oh what's he done now?" When he was told, he turned around and said, "Oh that lad 's making me ill"

You would have thought Scott would have learned from mistakes he's made in the past but he continued making them but in the process, he continued to give us all a damn good laugh.

It was on a window replacement scheme when Scott was stung again, a similar situation as before only this one a little more expensive.

Once more, a van rolls up on site and the driver then began asking the lads in the vicinity if they want to buy any TV's.

Again, Scott was on the scene and first to say, "I'll have them," not allowing anyone else make a shilling.

So, he was shown a new TV that was not boxed and the bloke said to Scott "I can't open another box else any other buyers will think they're second hand."

Scott had to go to the cash machine to get some money to pay for the TV's. Meanwhile the bloke unloaded them and left them on the grass verge. Scott returned and paid the man and off the van went. It was only later when moving the boxes to his car did he hear heard a jingling noise coming from one of the boxes. When he opened them all, each TV was in bits and broken parts everywhere. Scott had once again been stung big time.

He never did learn and was stung once more when a large transit van turned up full of carpets. The bloke from the van went to the site cabin with a sample book and began showing the lads.

Scott liked one of the samples and the bloke said, "Yeah! I have that one in my van in the size you just mentioned." Scott began asking how much the roll of carpet was.

The bloke said, "three hundred quid!"

The bloke had parked right in front of another vehicle making it difficult to look inside. Once at the van, the bloke asked Scott if that was the right one, Scott said, "Yeah that's the one".

Scott once again visited the cash machine to get his money for the carpet. When he returned, he did the transaction and was told to get a few of the lads to take it from the van.

As the van was parked right in front of another vehicle the driver said, "Get into position, bend down and put it on your shoulder whilst I drive the van away from the parked car and your work mates take the middle and the back."

As the van began to move forward Scott was standing there with a piece of carpet on his shoulder the size of a small rug, the van driver sped away leaving Scott done once again.

Andrew was an apprentice Plumber who was on the same site as me. Despite having little to do with the Plumbing section, every trade had their different day in the properties which were being refurbished. I quickly got to know the sparks and plumbers but to be an apprentice amongst those guys must have been hell.

Word got around site quicker than email and it wasn't long before I was listening about Andrews latest gullible task. One of the senior plumbers had sent Andrew to the store cabin on site with an order for four twenty-two mill fallopian tubes.

When he asked Pete the Foreman where in the cabin would he find these? Peter said, "Who's sent for these?" He shook his head and gave Andrew a smile and then told him he'd been set up.

When all the lads are together you find out the intelligent ones from the not so intelligent. We were gathered in the cabin for dinner when motor cars became the topic.

One guy mentioned he and his Father-in-law had removed and refitted a new engine in his car.

Another chirped up "did you use a block and tackle"? a delayed reply came "no we used one of those chains". Never a dull moment when in this job.

The Pranksters

Andy was a prankster but it did become his turn to be the victim of a prank.

The site was in Bolton where a Kitchen replacement scheme had begun. We had a great team who had been commended in a letter to the local newspaper from the previous job and received many compliments from satisfied tenants. It's always nice to be complimented on your work and we were very professional at what we did.

Andy was always smiling or laughing and was never miserable but he was a pest and was treated to a lesson of his own. One of the other lads had an idea to staple him to a fence, he realised he'd need a stapler so he got some Duct tape instead. He waited his time and enticed Andy over to assist him, it was then we all pounced. We held him until he was secure. We left him there but Andy was still laughing, we all wondered what we could do to make him not so happy. We left him there a little longer until one of the tenants came out who told us we were a bunch of rotters and we should untie him. Most of the tenants had seen what we did and saw the funny side.

Later into the contract, Andy was given the job of knocking a couple of bricks out for the waste pipe to go through, he was using his hammer and chisel when one lad suggested we threw some water on him. The Bathroom window was directly over his place of work, one of the lads took a bucket upstairs and half-filled it, the window was a side opener which enabled a full bucket to fit through. I do believe most of the other lads had taken up position in the bedroom to get a full view. The bucket was tipped and poor Andy got a soaking, he still laughed, though.

Michael Meadows was a young joiner just out of his time and was also a joker but a good hard working lad. Michael was used on this job for putting the finishing touches to the kitchens and bathrooms. He fitted plinths on the kitchens and fitted the fixings on the new shower cubicles and toilet roll holders etc.

Michael and his Kitchen fitting work mate Chris were a pair of jokers and were always enjoying a laugh. This particular day, Michael attempted to make a selfie video of himself jumping up and down on a bed. A local Radio show was asking for listeners to send in their videos of this bed jumping and Michael was ready to send in his. Chris held the camera phone whilst Michael began jumping. On his second jump he collapsed the bed breaking three of the wooden laths and two back legs. This was another job for Chris who ended up making three new laths and repairing the rear legs, not too sure if the tenant ever found out.

One of the most disgusting pranks I witnessed was on a kitchen and bathroom replacement scheme in Blackburn when one person who will not be named, denied all knowledge of his infamous stunt.

During a lunch break, one of the plumbers was installing a new bathroom suite which resulted in a bit of inconvenience for the tenants of the house. He'd got the bath installed and was in the process of connecting the toilet when it was time for dinner.

During lunch-time everyone went into this property to eat their sandwiches and enjoy a bit of banter. It was only after lunch when everyone went back to their place of work did this plumber find out what was in store for him. After returning to the bathroom he came running downstairs shouting, "where is he where is he"? One of the lads heard him and ran to his aid. The plumber asked if they'd seen anyone enter the house during lunch break because someone had a crap on the toilet and it hadn't been fixed or plumbed in. Meanwhile, the tenant's daughter returned home and she went upstairs to see if anyone was about, she visited the bathroom and saw what was in the toilet. This plumber saw her and told her not to go upstairs but it was too late she'd already seen the mess. Plumber instantly told her it wasn't him and tried explaining what he thought had happened. Whether she believed him or not is another issue.

Whilst on the same site some shower cubicles were being fitted replacing baths. At the end of the day, Steven, who was a labourer, was meeting a girl in town and needed to be clean. He used the shower that had been fitted. He couldn't find a towel so he decided to go and look for something to dry himself on. As he walked through the bathroom door two young college girls were walking up the stairs as Steve was standing there in his birthday suit and for once he was speechless. He ran back into the bathroom and asked the girls if they could get him a towel. He got his towel and was lucky not to lose his job. I would have thought the girls would have reported the matter but each time they saw Steven on site they just laughed. Steven did tell the Foreman who gave him a rocket and told him not to do anything like that again.

A site in Blackburn paired me up with another plasterer whom everyone called Arnie. He was a weight lifter and was always drinking some type of milkshake substance as a substitute for his meals. Despite being a weight lifter he seemed to struggle to pick up a bag of plaster and this didn't go un-noticed.

One particular day, another lad who was working on site said to Arnie, "I bet you can't lift and hold a full bag of plaster above your shoulders."

"Course I can," said Arnie. We were all close to the cabin where the plaster and cement were stored. Without any messing around Arnie moved towards a new bag and began his lift. The hold had to be ten seconds with the plaster held above his head. Arnie took up position where his lift and jerk were to perfection and the lift was completed, all he had to do was hold it for ten seconds to complete the task. Arnie was in the hold position when this lad went behind Arnie and took out a Stanley knife and slit the bag. The entire contents covered Arnie from head to toe. I couldn't stop laughing and I hadn't any idea as to what this lad was trying to do. Arnie ran after him down the street looking like a flour grader giving everyone a good laugh. Arnie knew he was a prankster but fell for the trick. Asked if I had anything to do with it I just said, "not at all."

A central heating job in a nearby Town was underway when one of the Plumbers required a few items from the stores. So, they contacted Ian in the Stores to see if these items could be delivered soon. Ian loaded up the box van and took the materials to where they were needed. It was a warm day and a lot of the items such as the bath and toilet were on the grass verge and the driveway to the property.

When Ian arrived, he couldn't get the van onto the drive so was told to reverse and someone will guide him. One of the plumbers had a fancy radio which was also on the driveway. This lad decided to guide Ian but made sure he guided the wheels over the radio flattening it like something from a cartoon sketch. Everyone apart from Steve whose radio it was were laughing.

Steve said "you can get me a new one after that stunt"

There was a job to be done in London around 1990 or 91 the job was to refurbish an office block on the Isle of Dogs. Alf who was a contracts manager was paying double wages for the lads down there. It must have plagued him to pay this so he decided to cut the pay by 10%. Anyway, as it happens his 50th birthday came up and the lads got him a birthday cake and gave it him with 10% of it cut out!

Les was always joking and enjoying a laugh and was always ready spring the surprise.

The company issued the foremen and other certain members of staff with walkie-talkies because Mobile phones were costing a fortune and he thought these were the way forward. These walkie-talkies could only be heard via a loud speaker and people had to be careful as to what they said. One particular day, Les thought it would be funny to contact another foreman on another job elsewhere. Because they were a new toy Les wanted to try it out so he contacted Kev.

Les shouts down the device, "Alright Kev you fat Bastard"! a moment of silence occurred before Kev returned his comment, "Hi Les I'm in the cake shop".

Whilst at Trafford site the pranks continued on a daily basis, and no one was safe from the practical jokers.

A tall lad they called Tarquin was a joiner who stood six foot six and was a regular at the gym. The lads had been winding each other up all week so by the time Friday morning came, something had to give.

Tarquin had a wooden tool box that he made himself and because it was Friday he always liked an early finish and two pm was his usual time for leaving the site.

It was around half past one when Tarquin went into a property where a group of the lads were gathered. Tarquin must have vacated the room when one lad decided it would be a good time to screw his tool box to the floor. They removed all his tools and fixed four or five screws to secure it.

After a few mins Tarquin returned and said, "see you all Monday." He then went to pick up his tool box and the handle came off in his hand, tools went all over the floor and laughs rang out but Tarquin seemed to have taken it quite lightly.

Monday morning came and nothing was mentioned about Friday's little stunt! But once dinner time came Tarquin got his revenge.

Andrew, the plumber paid the price for his practical joke and revenge was imminent. They had been talking all morning about Tarquin's tool box and decided Andrew's punishment would take place this dinner time.

Somehow, a two by one piece of timber had been inserted in Andrews coat sleeves. A few of Tarquin's boys got hold of Andrew and put him in his jacket with the wood in the sleeves. Once the coat was on they got him to the floor and screwed him down, this is where they left him all afternoon until someone heard him shouting.

One of the companies I subbed contracted for came through an agency and the job was quite local to me. Some of the strangest characters worked on this site and no one was safe from pranks, even whilst you were working a few of the younger end didn't have any respect for health and safety.

It was another window replacement schemes but these were different, they were replacing the old sash windows which had wooden casing and needed a lot of plastering.

One day I was hard at work when I looked out the window and saw a pair of feet dangling from the scaffolding, I carried on but kept looking. I got a bit concerned and went outside, a young lad had been hung up by the hood of his jacket and left dangling there. I climbed the ladder to the first level where he was. This lad was cursing and swearing, "I'll get you all back". I asked one of the elder workers if he would give me a lift to get him down but even he was in on it. Apparently, the lad dangling from the scaffolding was being taught a lesson because of his pranks, which I had no idea of. I then found out his name was Robert but most called him 'slither'.

I soon found what this little whippersnapper was about when he bored a few holes in each and every bucket, I had. He must have done it whilst I was mixing plaster. I had gone inside the house to fill a bucket with water but left a trail of water all over the floor. I knew in an instance who had done it but I couldn't prove it.

I became more vigilant whilst on this site and became accustomed to lads running after this prankster. A new starter began who was a site labourer cleaning the scaffolding but he was a little slow, nice lad but he talked slow and rambled on and on.

After a few days, he kept mithering me, he'd sit down watching me whilst he gabbed away about virtually anything he could think of. Slither found out about this and turned his attentions to the labourer. During his lunch break, he found out he had a flask of soup, mainly vegetable which gave him some crazy ideas. The majority of the tenant's go out for the day whilst work is being carried out and this property had everything in the kitchen at Slithers disposal. I was having nothing to do with his next brainstorm and kept them both at a distance.

Slither came into the house where I was working and I instantly said to him, "get out of here before I throttle you." Slither said he wanted to use a blender to mix some food he'd brought with him. I began thinking what the hell is he up to. He disappeared off site for a while but we all found out what he had been doing later.

Dinner time approached and we all sat down, this labourer began to open his flask and pour some of the soup into the lid then dunked a piece of bread into it. Slither began howling and the majority knew he'd done something. Howls turned into screams and nearly all in the room were rolling over. I hadn't a clue what was so funny.

This Labourer began questioning his soup, he said, "There seems more veg in this one than the others and it tastes a bit different." Slither had left the room and it was only later in the day when I found out what he wanted the blender for. He's found a load of slugs and mixed them up and added them to this poor lad's soup, he was never told about this but he had suspicions.

Slither returned to one of the properties I was working in and that alerted my suspicions considering the tenant who was out. He was very quiet which suggested he was up to mischief. After a search, I couldn't find him so I presumed he'd left without causing any problems. Soon after the tenant arrived home and began making a brew. As she was in the kitchen I noticed the photograph of herself and husband on their wedding day had been drawn upon. Both had Moustaches and beards drawn by a felt pen. The lady handed me a cup of tea as I stood in front of the picture. She asked me to sit down whilst I drank it. I was a little apprehensive but I did move but she never noticed. It was only later in the day that she reported the incident to the Foreman! Brian must have known in an instance who it was because he never approached me.

Pranks continued to take place so I decided to call it a day as the antics became a little more annoying to a point that something serious would happen.

The foreman on this job was hardly ever seen and even his name was, "dangerous Brian"!

Elf n Safety

Health and safety has always been a major player for lowering the accidents which occur on site, but it has also been a pain for many as we found out.

I always used a beer crate as a hop up because as a plasterer it was easy to move around and took up less room than step ladders. Until recently my crate had been tolerated but the Health and Safety thought otherwise.

I was on a job in Bolton when I was told to stop using it and instead use one of the platform ladders which were bulky and difficult to manoeuver into small areas. I was also issued with a pair of fingerless gloves a hard hat and goggles. All these were issued with the thought of protection but not for comfort. All the big chiefs at the company were keen everyone wore them and were constantly reminding us of the safety aspects. I can understand the need to keep workers safe but this had gone too far. One of the chiefs happened to be a woman, she thought she was someone and threatened to confiscate my crate, no way was I giving her my crate.

I was patch plastering kitchens after the electricians had rewired. I wore my gloves, hard hat, goggles, and steel toe cap boots along with knee pads which I have always worn. Those gloves were a pain in the backside because they got wet making my hands sore. I looked like a spaceman with all that gear on.

So, there we were made to wear all the safety gear when the tenant of the house came into the kitchen wearing shorts, tee shirt and sandals asking if I wanted a brew! I'm sure you could imagine the scene if we told him to wear what we were wearing we'd never have got a brew.

The sparks had to use a cage scaffold just to reach the ceiling. This had to be closed whilst working and was like being encaged.

When ROK took over Durose & Goulay, what they were offering was quite incredible. Their aim was to make us the best-certified workers in the country by sending us on courses for topics like Manual Handling and working in tight spaces. One day we were told to assemble at a Hotel not too far out of Bolton where a bonding session would take place. We were divided into small teams and left to solve puzzles. Once we'd worked out how to complete them we were asked to repeat the process but this time against the clock.

A demonstration played by part-time actors would demonstrate the importance of Health & Safety. This was nothing we already didn't know. These actors would demonstrate the dangers of mobile phones whilst on scaffolding, to be honest, anyone using a phone whilst on a scaffold was a numpty.

Dinner time approached and one of the lads had a good idea, there was a pub attached to the Hotel and he thought it be an opportunity for a pint or two.

We had dinner first which was provided and ventured into the bar area. Steve liked a pint but so did I. After about four pints each we went back to where the action was. There was much more brain-washing in store for us.

At the end of the session we were asked questions whether we'd change our working habits after watching these demonstrations. I was asked what changes would I make to my working practices but my reply was not what the person asking the questions would have expected.

My reply was, "I ain't gonna do anything different because I am blessed with common sense and my area of work is safe unless some prankster invades it."

This woman was quite shocked by my reply and shouted out, "He's said he's not going to do anything different." A laugh rang out from the rest of the attendants.

Elf n safety used properly and sensibly is a vital factor for keeping workers safe, but there have been times when it has been an insult to some people's integrity all because certain folk possess no common sense whatsoever.

So, glad I don't have to put up with Elf & Safety again.

Snagging

One of the down sides of refurbishment jobs is snagging! Snagging is when the work has been completed and the property is ready to be handed over but there could be a hole or a plug socket the Electricians had moved or forgot to take out. I am always greeted with a snagging list and sometimes it can be a bit of a pain.

This particular contract was quite large where over a hundred properties would be fitted with new central heating and a full re-wire. One day I was given a snagging list as in one house I had missed plastering a small chase which was hidden by the position of the bed. The tenant of the property knew I was coming and he left a key with one of the neighbours as he wouldn't be back in time for my arrival.

I followed the instructions that the small chase was behind a bed. I took the dust sheets and placed them down, just then the tenant of the house arrived home and assisted me moving the bed to one side. He was a bloke in his 50s and lived alone. As we moved the bed a black vibrator came into view.

The bloke got a bit upset by this and began kicking it back under the bed, "It's not mine, not mine," he kept saying.

I told him it was ok and nothing to be ashamed of. As the bed moved a few more feet I exposed a batch of magazines.

"Ooh those are not mine neither," but once again I said it was fine and no need to be embarrassed. The bloke ran downstairs and I never saw him again that day. Once I'd completed the work I handed the key back to the neighbour who asked me why he ran out of the house so quickly. I didn't say what I had found but she smiled broadly as if she knew a thing or two.

Working on this site were a couple of Central Heating fitters who were a law unto themselves. They got away with murder because they were simply the best at their professions. These two likely lads, Alan and Ian could fit a full central heating system in a day with hardly any snags. They also were a pair of devils who were always looking through the knicker drawers especially if the tenant was an attractive female.

One day one of the lads went to pay Ian & Alan a visit. What he saw he couldn't stop laughing, both were wearing a pair of briefs and other frilly items of underwear, this got them the nickname of the Panties Men. Even when tenants returned home, they always mentioned to her that they liked her underwear!!! I don't believe anyone else would have got away with what they did and said. It was never a dull moment when those two were on the same site with me.

Whilst working for BS Heating, most of the jobs were on a price. A pair of Plumbers had complained that their prices were not enough to feed their families. Dave who was the senior Estimator decided to pay them a visit on site and took with him two tins of beans just for a laugh but the two plumbers didn't see the funny side.

Dave was chased up the Street by these two Plumbers and it was only the intervention of the Foreman that prevented Dave from getting a good hiding.

Arrested

Working on social housing schemes has some funny moments but it can also place you in some dangerous situations.

I was Sub Contracting for a local company at the time and my job was to remove the grille coverings then plasterboard and skim making the wall neat and tidy. The warm air units had been replaced by storage heaters and the air ducting was no longer needed. This particular day, the job I had to do was on the seventh floor of a high-rise in Stockport. I collected my tools from my van and went about to do my normal day duties. These grill covers were screwed in place to the ducting but this one had clips which were a totally different fixing to those I had been used to. The front cover came off quite easily but what was behind it was another issue.

After removing the grille cover I found a stash of hypodermic needles along with small bottles and loads of small plastic bags full of dried leaves, all which I left in place. I finished plaster-boarding the gaps and then reported the find to the housing association.

Mobile phones were for the rich folk only then so other methods of communication were available to report this find. At the bottom of the stairs was a call button that allowed contact with the warden whom I spoke with via this intercom system. I told her about the find and that the police should be informed. Whilst I was downstairs I mixed a small bucket of plaster and took it to the flat. Around half hour later two Police Officers along with the warden came into the flat. I was sitting in the chair waiting for the plaster to set slightly to enable it to be trowelled smooth.

The Warden pointed to me and said, "That's him."

Well immediately I was grabbed and given my rights. These two Officers led me downstairs to the police van and took me to the Police Station, I'd already told them I was the one that found the hypodermics but they wouldn't listen. I couldn't even understand why the Warden didn't speak up for me but she was as thick as a Wigan butty.

After half hour of intense interrogation, I was set free. The two Officers realised they'd made a mistake and took me back to the flats. They spoke with the Warden who told the Police they didn't give her time to explain. I also had a right go at her. I returned to the flat where two other guys were mooching around but they wouldn't allow me back into the flat to complete my work. They gave me my tools and buckets and told me to leave. My guess would be they were from the drug squad. I often wonder if that Flat ever was completed.

Gash and the Basque

Once again Gary the Store person had another adventure, this time wearing Women's underwear.

This particular property was home to a woman around Forty-five years old who would leave underwear all over the house depending on which each trade was to go in. Knickers and bras would be left hanging from door handles and over the banister.

This particular day time had run out to finish the property so arrangements were made to be there the following day at 8am. Les told the woman he'd be there just after 8am.

She said, "If you're here before I go out I'll make you a brew and some toast because I go out at half past but I will be back around half past twelve."

The next morning tea and toast were ready and waiting. Linda said, "I'm off now but will be back at half twelve." So off she went leaving Les and Gary in the house to complete the jobs that needed completing.

Les went upstairs and found a pair of knickers hanging from the bathroom door and a Basque hanging over the wash basin.

As Les was fixing the shower curtain when Gary came into the house, he called, "Gash come up here and have a look at this."

Up came Gash and noticed the Basque hanging over the basin. Next thing Gash is trying to get into this Basque and says to Les, "Zip me up will you."

Les almost fell into the bath laughing. Being fascinated by these items of underwear left lying around, Gary began to take a closer look around. He looked in a cupboard and noticed a polystyrene head with a curly wig on it. Gash was already wearing the Basque but then tried on the wig and began looking in the mirror fancying himself.

As Gash was still parading around in this Basque, Les heard a car draw up outside the house, "Gash she's back"

"She can't be, she said half twelve."

Les insisted, "she's back!"

Gash took off the wig and placed it back on the polystyrene head and closed the cupboard door and then asked Les to unzip the Basque.

Les replied with a sly, "No!"

Linda then was at the bottom of the stairs and must have heard all laughter and decided to come up the stairs. Gash somehow managed to get the Basque undone and just as the bathroom door opened gash threw the Basque in the direction of the basin and it somehow landed in the same place as Linda had left it. Linda then began asking why are you both laughing, she said, "that's a dirty laugh, what have you been up to?"

Panties & Nicknames

Some of the houses on that contract were having a full central heating installed. The two lads installing the system were quick and good at what they did. They also had a way with words and got away with almost anything.

One lunch break I visited the property where Ian and Alan were working. The tenant of the house had just returned from a shopping trip with her friend and both carried bags containing the goodies they had bought.

Alan who was a right little devil asked the girls to show him what they had purchased. They took from the bag a few pairs of briefs and a satin nightie.

"I demand you go and try those on, come on let's see if they suit you at all." This took both women by surprise but Alan insisted once again.

"Oh alright then," said the girls who disappeared into another room.

By George one of them did go and try them on which left Alan for once speechless. I was in stitches laughing at Alan's reaction as the woman stood there parading in just a pair of briefs and a see-through gown. The word got around the site quicker than the pony express and shortly after we were joined by the labourers, electricians and other site personnel.

It's always been custom to look through the knicker drawer whenever work commenced in a property especially where a nice attractive lady lived.

A window replacement scheme was underway and everyone on site knew where the attractive ladies resided and it's usually at these houses where the knicker drawers come under close scrutiny.

The window fitters were at work in this particular property when one of the lads below shouted up, "Have a look in the top drawer, left-hand side of bed."

I can't remember the lad's name who was upstairs at the time but he began to open the drawer but found it was stuck. He tried again giving it a little more effort without much luck. The cabinet was one of those from Ikea and made from chip board with a laminate finish. One final pull saw the entire cabinet fall to bits. Knickers and other items of clothing lay scattered across the floor.

"Oh shit," could be heard from the street and a shout to one of the joiners asking for him to come and help him re-assemble this drawer unit.

One of the joiners paid him a visit and tried repairing the cabinet but was more interested in the contents of the drawers. Like others, he stole the show by trying on a pair of knickers and a bra and began to parade himself in front of the opening where the new window would be fitted. Word got around the site after this and some of the tenants decided to tape up their knicker drawers and even put locks on them.

Another woman on the same site told the plumbers all her knickers and other goodies were in the top two drawers just to save them time looking.

It was only my second day on this particular site. There were a few lads I knew from previous sites and a few I didn't know. I decided to have my dinner in the site office where most gathered to eat their dinners and have a brew.

The conversation was about football and was quite interesting to me. Bolton had Beaten Man United at Old Trafford and many of the lads were Man U fans.

Another lad entered the room and began telling us when it's our turn to go into number 34, take a look in the top left-hand drawer, at the side of the bed.

The conversation changed when one lad chirped up, "I was in there yesterday you could have told me then".

The intrigue got the better of a few and soon after dinner they visited the property and began having a rummage through the drawers.

During the afternoon brew we were all gathered and again the conversation was about number 34 and the knicker drawer. They were in a discussion comparing this drawer contents compared with others they had been through when the woman in question appeared at the door! She must have heard the conversation and began to question our activities in her property. She only came around to give the lad working in her house a key because she had to go somewhere and wouldn't be back before they left the site.

She said to everyone, "Don't bother looking in that drawer, if you're into knickers take a look in the spare room, there's another set of drawers in there containing all my special underwear." As she was leaving she said, "happy hunting"

The key was left on the table and a mad dash for it looked like a rugby scrum, about six lads made their way to number 34.

Some of the nick names we get christened with are not to be repeated and I managed to get one of my own. When I sub-contracted for BS Heating, Alan and Ian gave me a name which lasted throughout my time with them. I had long curly hair and a slight moustache, all that was missing was a shell suit. I got Christened with the name "Terry," one of the scouser characters from the whacky Harry Enfield series. Everyone I met called me Terry, even when I had a haircut the name stuck with me.

Another lad called Mark from BS who was a contracts manager was very regimental but liked to socialise with his fellow-workmates. A group of them were regulars on paint ball assault courses and he got the name Sergeant Slaughter because of his ruthlessness during the game.

Some of the characters I've met had unusual nicknames and one guy I worked with had been christened with a classic.

Will was a Joiner by trade and a mild-mannered bloke but he got angry once and one of his fellow workers renamed him Will der Beast!

The first time I met Will was outside a property which required a ceiling repair after water damage. Will was on hand to fix some skirting boards and fix a new door and casing. Both of us were waiting outside this house as the tenant had just got out of bed and would only let us in once she was dressed.

During the course of the Morning, another Tradesperson turned up and said to Will, "Morning Beast"! Will never said much and got back to his job.

I asked this other lad what he actually said to Will. He replied: "He's Will der Beast"?

I started on another site where Will was the Joiner and every morning the lads would come into the office and one by one they'd greet Will, "Morning Beast!"

This time he said in a mild voice, "Now let's have less of this Beast"!

I was told on one site that everyone began to shout Beast! Beast! Beast! Which turned into a full foot stomp with the entire office full shouting Beast!

Each time I was on the same site as Will, all he ever was called by was Beast.

Between jobs, the company always kept us busy. I was given the job of storeman driving the pick-up.

One day I was asked to go to the stores and see Cack for a pair of doors that were needed for one of the properties in Blackburn.

I said, "Who the hell is Cack"?

Kev just said, "You'll find out when you see him." This guy got the nickname because he wore baggy track suit bottoms and it looked like he'd done a dollop in them.

I can remember being sent to another site in Blackburn.

The site manager said, "Adder's the foreman and this is the address for the site office." The following day I made my way to Blackburn. I found the address and asked one of the lads who the foreman was.

"Adder" he said.

"Yeah I know his nicknames Adder but what's his real name?"

"Oh, it's Andy." I found out later why they called him Adder. It was because he looked a bit like Rowan Atkinson from the TV series Black Adder. I was thinking the guy looked like a snake or was a sly bloke, turned out he was neither and was a decent guy.

The House of Dung

Wigan never ceased to amaze especially this particular council estate. The contract was a window and door replacement that would bring the housing estate to standards of others. Even the concrete shelter would see a double-glazed unit installed and a more modern door fitted.

Roy was the Foreman, he liked to puff away on his pipe but got stressed quite often when problems occurred. He was very regimental in his way and wasn't scared of rollocking anyone, if they stood out of line. He wasn't a very politically correct bloke and told it as he saw it.

Some characters lived on this estate along with many shady ones. It doesn't take long before we stumbled upon them. Mark Jordan and Neil Bannister also known as Jordy & Banny were fitting the windows and their friends Ian Dunne and Mark Anglesea also known as Dunny and Angy were installing the lintels prior to anything else. These windows were being installed four inches further forward leaving a gap that required plastering. Jordy and Banny were a pair of butchers who removed the old wooden windows with brute force leaving the reveals hanging off. The head just had a massive gap which needed stuffing with rock wool or foaming up prior plastering. I made a deal with Banny and Jordy that they foam the cavities prior leaving the house which made my job quite easy and more straight forward.

I was warned the day before regarding this particular house which I was to plaster, as it was a bit of a smelly place and was home to three dogs. I arrived just after eight am and was greeted by a dog, this dog didn't have much fur and was covered in scabs and sores, the lady of the house told me not to be frightened as once I'd stroked it and gave it a kiss it would leave me alone, urrgghh..... no way would I even touch it.

It was usual practice to place dust sheets from the entrance and virtually everywhere where I would be working. Some properties, the dust sheets were cleaner than the floors they were to cover and this house was no exception. As I was walking to the kitchen a voice said, "be careful in there" I found out why on entry. There must have been a dozen dollops of crap and puddles of doggie pee it also stunk like hell. It was like playing hop scotch trying to get near the kitchen window. Some folk don't have a care in the world. I asked politely if this shite could be scooped up. In came the lady of the house, shovelled it up and asked me if I would like a brew? Erm no thanks.

Upstairs wasn't much cleaner and a young lad who was in bed went berserk when I took down the dark blanket nailed to the wall covering the window. Beside the bed was a tray of cat litter full and soaking wet along with another couple of turds presumably from the dog at the bottom of his bed. How this guy drops off to sleep with that besides his bed is another issue. The small room stunk like camels had visited during the night and the main bedroom was just as bad. The dust sheets I used were cleaner than the sheets on the bed.

After I had done the work in there I threw a couple of dust sheets in the skip.

At that point Roy, who was the Foreman came out of the Site office cabin. "Oi, what the hell you doing throwing them away, those can be laundered"? When I told him which house I'd been in, he told me to throw the others in the skip as well.

Dunny and Angy were two big lads both over sixteen stone but quite fit as they played Rugby league each weekend. Angy was Dunny's assistant as they were the only two in front of everyone on site. They fitted the new lintels prior the new PVC windows fitted. Angy would knock out the bricks, mix the mortar and clean the bricks ready for re-use.

It was the Friday leading up to Christmas and the site was cleaning down ready for the break so a few went for a pint. A new Chinese had opened not too far away in town and the shop had a special offer of all you can eat for a certain amount. Dunny and Angy, Banny and Jordy went to pay the place a visit. It was around 2pm and the shop was quite full but enough room for four more. They paid their money and ordered the food. Once they had polished off what they had they ordered more chicken wings and chicken breasts. Still they were hungry and asked the waiter over who told them thank you for your custom!

"No said Dunny we want some more chicken legs please."

The waiter went to see the manager who politely came over and told them surely they'd had enough.

"No," said Angy. We are still hungry."

One of the staff came over pleading with them to leave. The lads were a little cheesed off by this and quoted that it did say all you can eat for a certain price. They left with a huff and mentioned they wouldn't be returning.

Gasher the Smasher

Roy, who was the Foreman, was always getting stressed but he got even more stressed with the knowledge that on the next site he had Gash has his store-man. Roy would puff away at his pipe and the puffs got quicker the more stressed he was.

Gash was a liability at times but he was dedicated to what he did during the hours of work and tried his best not to annoy or upset anyone.

The company had a shop in Bolton that was being turned into flats so Roy sent Gash to pick up some materials for the job. Gash seemed to have been gone ages and Roy began wondering where he'd got to. Smoke was now bellowing from the pipe with Roy saying, he'd only sent him for a few lengths of three by two. The next thing, a loud noise, *crash clatter,* could be heard. There was a car park at the side of the building with a sign *Max Headroom* six foot six inches. Gash had driven onto the car park but it was the wood, which was higher than the pick-up that demolished the headroom barrier and smashed the pieces of wood to bits.

As you can imagine, Roy was not at all happy and said to Gash, "Oh, Gary what have you done now you great buffoon?"

Gash was always bumping the pick-up and everyone could tell when this happened just by the look on Gary's face.

This day Gash had gone to the chip shop for his dinner but when he returned he parked the truck in the exact place where he was before.

One of the lads noticed Gashes face and happened to tell Roy, "I think Gash's had a bump. I can tell by his face."

So, gash got out of the pickup and went into the office cabin to eat his dinner where Roy said to him, "Have you had another bump you, daft buffoon?"

"Sorry Roy, but yeah I've had another bump."

"Do you not look where you're going at all?" asked Roy.

Gash had reversed into a Mini but said, "It wasn't there when I went to the chip shop."

One morning on a window replacement job, Gash loaded the windows for two properties onto the back of the pick-up. The cabins were close to the site office so everything could be properly monitored. All of a sudden, a massive crash smash could be heard; it was Gash again. He'd set off in the pick-up with around fifteen double glazed windows but forgot to secure them before driving off. All the windows were smashed to bits.

Every dinner time, Gash would get hot water from a certain property so he could have a brew. Gash also took Les Potters flask to be filled.

Johnson Fold in Bolton was the social housing estate where a selected number of properties was being gutted and refurbished. There were walls to be knocked down and new ones built which were free-standing.

This particular lunchtime, Gash had already got his flask filled with hot water but somehow ignored Les.

Les gave Gash a bollocking, but was finding it difficult to keep a straight face saying, "Where's my flask?"

Gash was moaning saying, "I'll go and get it."

As it was the paving flags had been removed and were to be lowered. Planks were put down for a walkway. Because it had been walked upon all morning the planks had moved to the edge which was resting on the steps and Gash was to be the unlucky one because when he stepped on it, the plank collapsed sending the flask flying and ending up smashed.

Gash was moaning, "My leg, my leg."

Les said, "What about your leg? What about my flask you idiot?"

So, Gash rolled up his trouser leg and his skin had been grazed. "What you going to do about that?"

Les quickly replied, "What you gonna do about my flask?"

So, Gash was hobbling about and came inside one of the properties and just happened to lean on a free-standing wall that had just been built. All the lot came tumbling down. Any other company and Gash wouldn't have lasted two minutes.

The Phantom of the Opera

Every so often you'd meet a character you would never forget and Lloyd was no exception.

Lloyd was a Joiner and a gentle Giant who was always singing Opera. No matter where on site Lloyd was working, you could hear him. Luciano Pavarotti was nothing on this guy.

I was sitting in my car having a brew when all I could hear was Lloyd singing some Elvis song in front of a window. The old lady of the house came out wagging her finger at him telling him to be quiet. When Lloyd was on site there is no such thing as quiet.

I first met Lloyd on a site in Wigan. His first words were, "Right, what's your name?"

I told him who I was and the reply came, "Pleased to meet you. I'm Lloyd Pugsley, Rugby League legend, friend to the stars, put it there." He said that to everyone he met.

Kev was foreman on this job and he was always saying to Lloyd. "Keep the vocals down a little, will you." Lloyd never bothered and continued regardless. Never a dull moment on this site.

Whilst I was working in a property, Lloyd just nipped in for a chat. He said to the old dear of the house, "Eeee! love, what's that plastic thing Golfers put their ball on?"

The lady would then say, "Tee."

"Aye that's right, two sugars and a little milk in mine please and don't put too much butter on the toast else the egg will slide off."

His one liners were so funny.

A job broke out up in the Lancashire hills near Rossendale. Lloyd had been made up to foreman. It was another window replacement job but Lloyd continued to help the lads with the fitting. There would be a small amount of plastering which was enough to keep me busy for the duration. Because of the distance, Lloyd had use of a van and picked me up each morning along with another two lads.

The journey to work each morning was never dull even if the weather was. We'd arrive on site and Lloyd would open the cabins and the lads would load the windows for the job.

This particular house, where the windows were being fitted, Lloyd was already in fine voice.

An elderly Lady said to Lloyd, "You should have been on *Opportunity Knocks*."

Lloyd replied by saying, "I already won that."

The elderly lady was saying to everyone she knew, "do you know that man there he won *Opportunity Knocks*."

Her Husband was always walking around the house moaning it was cold.

"Get out 't road, you dithery old bugger and get the kettle on," said Lloyd jokingly. That was the sort of character he was.

Whilst on a Wigan site Lloyd was in top form. I can recall visiting Lloyd whilst he was fitting new windows but I needed to inspect the damage. Lloyd was quite a brute when removing the old windows which left a lot of plastering.

The sound of singing directed me straight to the property that Lloyd was working. I was greeted with a rendition of *Barcelona*, then a few words to the house tenant.

"Get that kettle on for this lad. Can't you see he's gasping." I just shook my head because Lloyd was Lloyd.

When the Tenant returned from the kitchen, Lloyd said, "Denn, listen to this! Me and this woman would make a cracking duo." Lloyd burst out in song and waited for this elderly lady to join in. "Come on, you silly old bat, sing like you did before." She was a bit shy but she did eventually burst into song singing *Barcelona* on an equal level to Montserrat Caballe.

After the lady had left the room Lloyd said, "I'm trying to humour her because I broke a vase that was on the window shelf and she's not noticed it's gone yet."

Sadly, Lloyd is no longer with us, he is missed by his Colleagues Friends Wife & Family.

Snacks away

It's amazing really, how different parts of the Country have different references to certain food items. Some of the lads who worked in Blackburn would have learned a different name for one of their favourite bread snacks. A visit to a chip shop nearly turned into a full-scale argument.

When I arrived on the Blackburn site I was shown the properties which needed plastering. I was also warned of Jimmy who was one of the labourers. Jimmy would argue for Britain and wouldn't let any argument die until the others gave up.

I even vouched for and defended Jimmy when we visited a chip shop in Blackburn.

He asked for, "Chips, peas and gravy and a Barm cake."

The guy behind the counter said they didn't sell Barm cakes! This baffled both us because there was a full plate of them on display. We pointed to them and told him they had some there on that plate? #

The guy serving us said, "Ahhh, you mean Tea Cakes."

I said, "No they're Barm cakes because Tea Cakes have currants in them." This guy wouldn't have it and asked a few locals waiting in the shop to correct us. Well, this sprung Jimmy into action who began to hurl abuse at the guy behind the counter. He told us to leave immediately. I'd only just met Jimmy as it was my first day on this site.

Once outside the shop, we both shouted, "Barm Cakes." We got neither our chips nor Barm cakes.

Now Rochdale is different again. Their version of Barm Cakes are baps and in Ashton Under Lyne they call them Muffins?

On another site Mike Mooney visited a pie shop, it was a hot day but a pie would have done fine. When it was Mike's turn to be served, he said, "I'll have a pie and a wasp."

The lady serving got the pie and asked Mike what else did you ask for? "Erm, a wasp."

"A wasp?"

"Yes," said Mike. "There are many in the window."

The woman serving smiled and said, "The zapper isn't working, so I do apologise."

It's surprising that the further south you travel the pies are not as good. No doubt I stand to be corrected on that but I believe it to be true.

We had a site in Macclesfield and could we get a decent pie? No we couldn't. Everything in that shop was flaky pastry and greasy. The lads searched for a decent pie without much luck.

One of the lads visited a chippy, returning back to the cabins saying, "They don't know what pey wet is."

Now not many would know what pey wet is. Just to educate a few, pey wet is the water from the peas.

Whilst working in Macclesfield we did a test on the residents asking them their terminology for certain foods. I asked what they called a Barm Cake in Mac? None of them knew what a Barm cake was. Their interpretation was a bap. One of the lads asked if they ever had Parkin Cake and Black Peas? We asked about twenty tenants in Mac and no one had ever heard of Black Peas or Parkin.

Fifty Shades of Day

Chatting up women on site was outlawed but it did happen and quite often.

One site that we worked on in Wigan Metropolitan Borough was rife with women finding many of the workers an attraction. These women were very accommodating in more ways than one. Many, were divorced and lived alone and some had children. Reports got around of many affairs which left a few of the women complaining that they had not been approached.

One particular day, a few of the lads were gathered in the cabin having a brew when a dwarf-like lady from one of the houses that were being refurbished stepped inside the cabin and began shouting! "Hey, what's all this about, everyone copping off whilst I'm not."

A few of the lads looked at each other and thought oh no were not going there.

Suddenly one of the lads said, "Well if it's a quick one you're after, then I've got fifteen minutes."

The most bizarre sight I ever witnessed was on a site in Irlam which was south West of Manchester. This was a window and door replacement scheme and involved rebuilding a few garden walls.

Each day we would report to the site office to discover which was of the houses were to be done and wait for instructions. We always had a brew before setting about our daily tasks.

I was to go where the windows were fitted the day before and there was always damage to the reveals which usually required beading and plastering. I was given the key and off I went. The lady of the house was in her thirties and very attractive, she seemed a business type girl who worked till late, we only saw her first thing in the morning before nine am as she must have worked in the City. It was always courteous to knock but this time, there was no answer so I presumed she'd gone to work. I took some dust sheets with me and placed them before each window and then took some upstairs. I went into the bedroom and unravelled a dust sheet, I knew instantly I wasn't alone by the heavy breathing coming from the bed behind me, as I turned around there was the lady of the house on top of the bed naked as a jay bird with a bloke in a compromising situation. I was stunned and began to walk out when she croaked "It's ok...... we've nearly finished do what you have to do!! I went back downstairs and brought my buckets and tools and the building materials I would need and put them in the garden. A bloke came out of the front door, got into a car and sped away down the street.

The lady of the house casually came up to me and said, "Feel free to make yourself a drink but don't forget to lock up!!" Some have no shame at all.

Some women make it obvious they fancy a certain member of the workforce and go all out to show it. It happens on every site but some of the lads are married and class it as an extramarital affair, others are single and actually fall in love.

A Kitchen replacement site in Bolton was to be our place of work for at least six months. As per usual, everyone weighs up who lives where, who is single and who is divorced? Carl was a Joiner who along with another joiner fitted the kitchens and fixed new skirting boards etc. A young lady living alone was an occupant in this particular house. She took a shining to Carl and he seemed to be spending a little more time in this property than the others. Living in close proximity were an elderly couple, they seemed to know everything about everyone and their property was re-named the `Watchtower.` One morning the lady from the 'watchtower' visited the site office which was one of those metal Portacabins, and mentioned to the site supervisor that the lads doing the work were very conscientious because the joiners car was on site till well after ten pm this particular night. Whether this lady was trying to get a message over or she was totally vague we'll never know. Carl did get a ribbing about his evening escapades.

A two-storey group of flats needed Kitchens replacing and this property in Bolton was more like a warehouse for Anne Summers than anything else.

The property had been surveyed and the tenant had her choice of kitchen design, she was also told of the slight disruptions she would encounter which would last around a week.

After the old kitchen was removed and the walls stripped down to the plaster the electricians were to re-wire it and needed access to the main consumer unit. The tenant had left a key with Mike at the site office as she went to work around eight am. The sparks entered the house but found the cloak store room was locked and this is where the consumer unit was located.

No one really knew much about the lady of the flat, apart from the first day when she visited the site office as instructed when the job began. She was a small lady in her late thirties early forties and wore visual aids. This type of lady would be the last you would imagine being into bondage.

The sparks had to enter this room else the work couldn't go ahead. Fortunately, Fishy who was one of the sparks had a knack of unlocking doors. Once this door was open they had a shock. There were all types of sexy uniforms chains and other gadgets that made the mind boggle. As soon as this was found everyone there had to vouch not to tell Eddie. Now Eddie was a right character who was into this sort of stuff and would have had a ball in this dwelling. Even young Michael was dancing around dressed in a black satin gown with a pair of small lady's briefs on his head.

Eddie was a plumber who didn't care what folk thought of him. He was a member of a Swingers club but was always after the ladies on the site.

We were working in Blackburn where a full kitchen replacement scheme was underway. Our job was to re-plaster the entire kitchen after all the old plaster had been removed. The lady of this property wasn't really bothered what she said or showed us. This girl had a port-folio book of her naked and was always showing the lads who were working there. Eddie found out that a book of such was being shown. It wasn't long before he showed up at the house and demanded to see the photos. Another woman was there at the time who took a shine to Eddie and it wasn't long before he was spending quite a bit of time in her property.

Many of the women on these sites would have scared a police horse.

Tales from the Bathroom and Bog

Some of the properties we have worked in have been disgusting to a point of refusing to go in and undertake the work. Every social housing estate has a few properties that need fumigating but some are even worse.

On a job in the Wigan Metro area, PVC double glazed windows were being fitted and needed a bit of plastering, once the old ones had been removed. By doing this it meant that I'd have to enter every room in the house. The lads who had been working at this particular property mentioned to me that it was rather smelly so wear a dust mask.

The following day I knocked on the door and the stench hit me as soon as it opened. I had to turn my head and I'd not even gone in. I got the dust sheets and began to place them beneath each window except the toilet room. This was separate from the bathroom but the bowl seemed full as if the flusher wasn't working. The bedrooms weren't much better as the pillows and sheets were grey and looked as if they hadn't seen clean water for over a year. The floor was used as a wardrobe and the curtains full of dust and there were more spider's webs than Hammer Horror Films.

I quickly ran downstairs and began to mix some plaster but was intercepted by the tenant who asked me if a plumber was on site and if so could they have a look at the toilet. Unfortunately, there was no plumber onsite but there was a young labourer who was always looking for something to do. I asked this young lad if he knew anything about toilets, he said "leave it with me"

As I was plastering up around the new windows this lad came in and said he would sort that out in no time and asked me if he could borrow a bucket.

I said to him, "I hope you're not emptying the contents of the bog into my bucket." Next thing this lad was upstairs when I heard a loud "urggggg." He'd poured a full bucket into the bowl and it overflowed and there were turds and paper everywhere, one even came bouncing downstairs.

The woman of the house gave the lad a bit of a roasting saying, "I've tidied up today and now you're making a mess!" Believe me, that house could not have got into any more mess than what it was already in.

On the same estate, I was warned of another smelly property and thought it couldn't be any worse than the last one I worked in. I visited the house where the windows were being fitted and told the two window fitters they were brave entering this place.

One of them said, "It's your turn tomorrow."

Whilst in the property, they'd sprayed the house with a tin of air-freshener purchased from the corner shop but when the woman returned from where she'd been she said to the window lads, "Urgh, what's that horrible smell?" Needless to say, they get used to their own environmental pongs.

A Senior moment

One good point about working amongst the senior citizens is you can't predict them. Some are forgetful others just worry about the disruptions they endure.

Whilst working on this housing estate on the outskirts of Oldham, my job was to re-plaster kitchens walls where the electricians had re-wired and to make the walls good where old tiles had been removed. New kitchen units were replacing the old decrepit ones and this was another good job for myself, nothing strenuous but enough to keep me occupied until leaving time.

Most the time the tenants were taken out whilst the messy work was taking place so they faced no problems with cooking and making cups of tea.

After a few weeks of this job the Foreman asked me if I could just return to one of the properties that had been finished to patch plaster where an old socket had been removed. I went to this property and knocked on the door but I never got a response. I knocked again but it seemed as if no one was home. Just as I was about to return to my vehicle I saw a slight movement in the frosted panel, it was only a slight movement but it did seem as if someone was home. I waited what seemed aged for this figure to open the door, finally, it opened. It was an elderly Gentleman who answered the door. He had two walking sticks and a hearing aid plugged into his ear. I told him I was the plasterer and had come to patch the hole where the Electricians had removed a socket......

A silence occurred then the Gentleman said in a dithery voice, "Ooh I don't know, I'd better go and ask my Mum"!!!!! The next person to arrive at the door was indeed his Mum who looked younger and was more active than her Son. Once inside she spoke about him as if he was a little boy. I couldn't stop laughing.

The French Dancing Babe

Nicknames are common in the building trade and a few are unrepeatable and could offend. Others are christened with names ending in the letter (Y) but one lad was re-named "The Dancing Babe," strange name for someone working on site.

Dave Pasquille had a tendency to get things mixed up quite often and one occasion he was having a conversation with the site storeman who was into computers in a big way. Peter the storeman was telling Dave that he had a new screen saver which featured dancing babies as shown on a TV programme by the name of 'Allie McGraw.' Dave came away a bit puzzled by the conversation he had had with Peter saying, anyone putting dancing babies on their screens must be a *peedlofile*. He got that totally wrong and couldn't pronounce the word properly.

Dave was always talking to the residents. Most must have thought he was nuts! Dave would say to people passing in his French accent, "Do you think the French accent is so sexy?"

One of the lads called Lee got hold of Dave's ID picture and gave it to Peter who made a picture of the dancing babies with the middle one having Dave's head on it. This was really funny so we put the picture up in the office where everyone could see it. They all had a good laugh apart from David who said they were a bunch of halfwits.

Dave was known from then on as the Dancing Babe and whenever that name was mentioned you knew it was Dave.

Another occasion was when chimneys needed rebuilding in Farnworth. Graham Dibnah, who was Fred's Brother, and Lee Dickinson were on the roof to do the rebuilding and Dave was meant to be sending the materials up to us by way of a Ginny wheel. The trouble was Dave had disappeared and the lads were up on the roof with no gear. About an hour later he reappeared whereupon Graham and Lee wanted to know where the hell had he been.

Dave mentioned he'd been in the house over there with the plumbers and the tenants had two iguanas. There's one on the back of the couch at it! Then he gave us a display of his version of the movements of an iguana which was very strange.

Dave was on a job in Leigh labouring where a pike was being rebuilt. Dave got talking to a couple of local girls who liked a drink and always seemed intoxicated. These two ladies were friendly and took a liking to Dave who told them he was French! And that his name was Gaylord Pasquelle and that he was gay.

These two women actually believed him and said to Dave, "Are you a giver or a receiver?" whereupon Dave replied sincerely and in all seriousness, that he was a giver because he wasn't having one of those up his backside. Lee couldn't keep his face straight.

Dave also told the women that because he was French he was also a good cook. The next thing the two women and Dave were in their kitchen next to where the work was going on. The windows and doors were all open and Lee could see and hear everything that was going on. All three of them were making one of Dave's special creations, tater-ash with his own ingredients thrown in.

All the lads working next door heard Dave say in his French accent, "All we need now is a clove of garlic." The woman whose house it was, was already plastered but did say there was no garlic, so Dave sent her to the local shop for some.

Dave was also asked by one of the women would he help her decorate her bedroom so Lee asked him if he was going to do it. Whereupon he replied that his wife would cut his balls off as he didn't do any decorating.

Grease Lightening

Some people like to enjoy the banter whilst on site but there are some really cruel ones who tend to go a bit too far.

There's always one person that is quieter than most and it's usually those that tend to bear the brunt of the jokes. Michael was a labourer who cleaned out the cabins and assisted anyone that needed a bit of help. He was always ready for his dinner and would be seen regularly nibbling on a sandwich or a chocolate bar. There were occasions when he'd join a group of us who got together in one of the properties where work was being carried out. He never bought any dinner whilst on site but always brought his own sandwiches.

One particular day, Michael dropped off his bag in one of the houses where we would gather for dinner. Steven was another labourer but was a right rascal who always got up to mischief on a regular basis. He noticed there was a bag and took a look, asking whose was this? He found out it was Michaels and proceeded to look what Michael was having for lunch.

He noticed a chocolate bar and some sandwiches that were wrapped up in cling film. He noticed something black oozing from the sandwiches and rubbed his finger on it. "It's black treacle," said Steven.

One of the lads said, "Put them back, you daft sod," but Steven thought otherwise. He disappeared for a while then returned with a tin of something, he then took out Michaels butties and began to remove the black treacle.

"What the hell are you doing?"

"Shhhh," said Steve leave this one with me.

We all gathered for dinner with most of us having used the local chip shop. Michael opened up his butties and began to take a bite, a chuckle from Steve rang out but no one was aware anything had been sabotaged. Michael continued to bite on his sandwich and by now his lips and mouth area were beginning to turn black and a slight twitch of his nose suggested all was not quite right. A few of the lads began laughing and then laughter turned into howls and it was at this point Michael spat out the partly chewed contents of his sandwich and demanded to know who was responsible for this. Michael wiped his mouth with the back of his hand and it left a black mark, he turned red and with a rage of anger and ran out swearing and cursing.

One of the lads asked what he'd put on his butties,

Steve said it was this that he'd found in the cabin, a tin of black axle grease. Michael was in the bathroom trying to remove the black substance but with not much luck.

We all told Steve to go and do one, else Michael would probably end up killing him.

After a full-blown argument, which almost ended up in a fight, they both shook hands and agreed to keep out of each-other's way. Steve got a right rollicking and was removed from that site never to be seen or heard of again.

Toilet Rolls & Teabags

A big contract was won this time in Wythenshawe which was allegedly the biggest council estate in the country. The properties here were having a full rewire and full central heating which would require quite a lot of plastering. The plumbers and electricians were the first tradespeople on site along with the labourers and the Clerk of works. The sparks were a group of four people including a labourer and an apprentice, there was to be a store-person and his assistant and the foreman.

It was a cold Monday morning and everyone descended upon the first house which should have been started a week earlier. This house was to be used as a pilot for the entire contract but snags and other problems prevented that. The lady of the house must have had the patience of a lord because her home was full of sparks and plumbers weighing up what would be required and wait to begin work. The Cable and radiators along with boiler and fittings had yet to be delivered and everyone was mystified. The tenant made everyone a cup of tea and one guy asked her if he could use the loo. Well, shortly after someone else needed to visit the loo and so on and so on until everyone had been. It was nine thirty and still no sign of the gear. The tenant made another brew and one of the gang had to use the loo again. By the time the cable and other equipment arrived, everyone had drunk four brews each and visited the loo twice.

It was approaching dinner time and the gear finally arrived. There had been problems collecting the equipment but to begin work at that time would not have been fair on the tenant so they all decided to call it a day and make an early start in the morning.

Tuesday morning, work finally began. It was really cold with sleet falling so everyone who was present on site made their way to this dwelling. Again, the tenant made everyone a brew and again everyone visited the loo.

At the end of the day the work was complete and the lady of the house announced she'd gone through six toilet rolls and a full box of tea bags. The foreman did ensure the lady would be more than compensated for her trouble and was presented with a large pack of Toilet Rolls and a large box of Tea Bags. The following day the house was re-wired ready for me the day after.

When I arrived the next day, I was told by the foreman to use the site Toilet and make sure not to ask the lady for a brew. When she told me about the previous day occurrences I couldn't stop laughing. She was such a great sport and we hoped everyone on this job would be of her kind. Plastering those houses was a nightmare as the sparks made holes everywhere and that was to be the bug bearing part of the job.

Wythenshawe turned out to be a good site which was home to some really great people. All were very accommodating but some in more ways than others. The foreman Steve seemed to have found a young lady at one dwelling and a few of the lads noticed he'd been visiting this particular house more than others. It was also noticed he wasn't in any hurry to leave the site and was always first to the office in the morning. When questioned, he denied all knowledge of the accusations and went about his work in an orderly manner. Steve had a shock after the electricians had visited that dwelling to rewire because the young lady took a shining to one of the sparks leaving poor Steve a bit miffed.

Calamitous

I recall working on an estate in Bury close to the Cemetery and football ground. This was another boiler replacement scheme and cavity wall insulation. There were other bits of jobs that required doing such as bricking up outside and inside where the old wall heater had been removed.

There was one house that was always difficult to get access to and it was at this property that my famous calamity occurred.

I always booked things down as to what I did and at which address. I did brick up the outside where the wall heater flu was removed but with no access to finish off inside.

This particular day, the foreman gave me a key to this property to enable me to block up the hole and make good inside by re-plastering the area. I had forgotten as I was deep in concentration on another property.

The Cavity Wall insulation team arrived and began to fill the cavity. I can always remember one of the insulation team mentioning that this property took much more insulating than the others. That day passed but the following morning I got a right rollicking from the Foreman and clerk of works for not blocking up inside that property. The lady of the house was on the phone when she got home from work after finding her bedroom full of small white particle fibres from the insulation. Clerk of Works instructed me to go around and sort it out.

I arrived at the house but the lady immediately offered me a brew which I accepted. She also asked me what I would be wanting for Dinner? That question baffled me a little. I followed her up the stairs to the bedroom and what I saw made me laugh out loud. I almost howled with laughter. The room was full of insulation because the hole in the wall was a lot bigger than usual after the wall heater had been removed. I now knew why she asked me what I would be wanting for dinner after I saw the mess.

I was relieved when a group of the insulation team arrived and began to remove all the stuffing that had been deposited because to clean that up on my own would have taken a few days.

Later, on the same site, I was asked to bore holes in the wall for a bathroom extractor fan to be fitted. I was shown where these fans were going to be placed and advised to use the core drill from the outside to reduce the dust etc. Drilling these holes was tedious and seemed to take ages.

This day was wet and windy which meant I would have to drill the hole from the inside. It was a messy process but a lot easier than standing on a ladder. I hadn't looked on the outside as there was limited space as to where these fans could go.

I sheeted the bathroom out and began to drill the hole. Normally the brickwork remains in the tube of the core-drill but somehow, this time, it didn't. It did seem to take ages but eventually I got through. There seemed to be something preventing the drill complete the hole so I gave it one almighty push then a massive smash could be heard. I heard a shout from the bottom of the stairs and went to see what the problem was. I went outside to the back garden and the first thing I noticed was a greenhouse with the glass roof smashed in.

"Oh, for god's sake," I shouted. On the wall, directly where I'd been drilling was a dummy burglar-alarm cover which I had knocked off subsequently smashing the greenhouse roof. Another fine mess I had got myself into.

My Young Friend

Not all the incidents which I experienced working on site were funny, there were also some sad moments which we encountered.

I will never forget the young boy who wouldn't leave my side. He clung to me like a leach.

I was sub-contracting for a firm in Leigh Lancashire when I was sent to a few jobs in the Wigan area.

The house I was working in had a boiler replacement and the old upstairs cupboard needed boarding out and skimming over. The tenant was a youngish woman with no evidence of anyone else living there apart from this young Boy. It was half term and the schools were closed.

I put the dust sheets down on the stairs and brought the tools and boards in. The young lad began talking to me asking questions about football and about myself. I asked him his name and I told him mine. Simon was only eight years old but quite knowledgeable about football.

It was Monday morning and I still had a match programme in my car from the weekend game when I went to watch Bolton when they played at the Old Burnden Park.

Before I begun to set about the task I went to the car and gave Simon the match programme in a hope he'd leave me alone to get on with the job. His Mum did remind him many times not to mither whilst I was working, but there was something about Simon I liked. He couldn't thank me enough for the programme, he showed it to his Mother and went out into the Street to show some of his friends. I did get the chance the cut the boards to fit before he came back and began talking about football.

During our conversation, Simon asked me what it was like to go to a football game because, he told me, his Mum wasn't interested in football and he had no one to take him. He also told me most of his friends had been to a game and he mentioned he was called names for never going to a game.

I felt really sorry for him and during dinner time I sat with his Mum whilst I had dinner. She told me he was hard work and demanded too much from her. I did get the impression she wasn't very good at parenting but I suppose being a single parent was difficult.

After dinner Simon was upstairs again trying to attract my attention, I wasn't bothered because the job not really difficult, just a bit fiddly. I actually became quite emotional when he told me he wished I was his Dad so that I could take him to a football match. If there was anything I could do I would have but that was the last game of the season otherwise I would have gladly taken him.

When I'd completed my work, I began to put the sheets and tools etc. back into the boot of my car. I saw Simon sitting on the stairs crying. I sat beside him and told him that if I was ever in the area working, I would call on him and have a chat. His Mother actually praised me for my patience and kindness, she did say that she would make an effort to take him to a football match when the new season began. I sincerely hope she was a lady of her word.

It was two years later when we returned to that estate and I was actually going to call on Simon but had to wait until after 4pm when he returned from School.

When I'd completed my work, I drove to the house and saw Simon playing football on the grass in front of his home with a few of his friends. He spotted me and came over. I was so pleased when he told me he'd been to see a football match but I was slightly disappointed when he said he'd been to see Manchester United.

When I think about this today Simon was eight in 1995, but I sincerely hope I had some kind on influence on him and his Mother.

No doubt he's turned out to be another closet Man U fan.

The Most Popular Room

A team of Electricians turned up at a property in Horwich. A man answered the door who told them he was going to work. He mentioned to the sparks that they should not enter a particular room. Again, the intrigue got the better of us so once all the tools had been taken inside and the dust sheets had been put down one of the sparks decided to go and take a look.

Once inside the room the sparks were met by a wall-sized picture of his wife in the buff. It didn't take very long before everyone on the site decided to go and take a look.

The Primitives

Whilst working on an estate in the Wigan area I came upon the most primitive family I think I'd ever seen. This estate was about two miles outside the town centre.

I arrived on site and made my way to the property which I would be working in. I was greeted by a pleasant lady who asked if I would like a cup of tea. Whilst the tea was cooling I put the dust sheets down and began to get my tools and buckets. Whilst I was unloading I noticed a few people gathering around this property. By the time I got to ask the lady about this a few more had converged outside.

I could hear noises coming from upstairs which I thought would be her Husband. The lady asked me had I come far?

I said," I live in Atherton." Now Atherton was only six miles from Wigan. She said she'd never heard of it.

I said, "It's near Leigh."

She said, "No I don't know where that is." Leigh is probably closer to Wigan than Atherton is.

I picked up the cup of tea and saw a young girl about eight or nine enter the room. I asked the lady why are all those people gathered outside your home?

She said, "My Daughter is going to Wigan in a minute."

My reply was, "so?"

The lady said, "Well she's never been before."

I asked her, "Are you new to the area?"

She just said, "No we have lived here for many years."

A woman and another young girl came into the house saying they were excited about going into town on the bus. This was their first time and a crowd had gathered to see them off?

Now some Wiganers are believed to be a bit primitive and this family was a prime example.

Postscript

I hope you enjoyed reading this book as much as I enjoyed writing it.

I would like to thank my wife Brenda for her patience whilst I remained in silence, with a laptop on my knee. Many say she deserves a medal for putting up with me over these years so when the chance comes I shall buy her one.

I'd also like to thank the other contributors to the book Les Potter, Mike Mooney, Ian Aston, Mark Jordan and Lee Dickinson.

A special thank you goes to Lionel Ross of i2i Publishing who came to my aid after a long process of seeking a publisher.